To my old pal Guillermo y Sweet Sue grace Catherine and Juan, with Love,

JS
June 14, 2014

My Curious Camera

The Coast-to-Coast Career Path
of a Restless Journalist

John Macauley Smith

© 2014
Crow Farm Books

My Curious Camera

The Coast-to-Coast Career Path
of a Restless Journalist

ISBN #9780615987989
Library of Congress #2014905830

Published by CROW FARM BOOKS, Veneta, Oregon
Printed by Clancey Printing Company, Eugene, Oregon

Layout by Paul Semonin
Cover Design by Chrissy Richards: lightboxgraphicdesign.com

If you wish to order additional copies, please mail a $35 check per book to
John M. Smith, 85316 Coyote Creek Road, Veneta, OR 97487.

Available through Amazon:

THE CROW FARM COOKBOOK:
A Manual of Food & Hospitality
with
Stories & Other Entertainment
by
Catherine & John Smith

(Second Edition © 2010)

Acknowledgments

My grateful thanks to Paul Semonin, aka graphic artist Violet Ray, for tirelessly overseeing the layout of this project and designing its pages. Special thanks also to Joey Blum for his always-helpful publishing guidance, and to my wife Catherine for her excellent and endless copyediting. Thanks also to Robert Hewlett, our technical guru, Annette Pfautz for her high quality digital scanning of the photos, and Chrissy Richards of Lightbox Graphic Design for expertly preparing these pages for publication. And to Marsha Shankman for her peerless advice, copy sleuthing, and encouragement. Without the efforts of each of these fine individuals, this project would never have left the gate.

Dedication

To my supportive wife and family

To my friends, old and new, who enrich my life

To those newspaper editors who took a chance on me

To the talented, hard-working staffers who taught me their craft

To my mentors who probably have no idea who they are

To those many talented and loyal volunteers who created
Aspen's community television channel out of thin air

And to my parents who gave me the freedom
to find and to follow my own path.

Introduction

While tidying up my "past" at age 80, I uncovered these photographs in storage boxes. The images were taken between 1959 and 1971 while I worked for various newspapers, free-lancing, and teaching, as well as exploring our amazing world.

All of these photographs were "grab shots" – un-posed photos taken with natural light using a 35mm camera. I have never considered myself anything other than an amateur photographer, and I did nothing that you could not do yourself. So, I encourage you to look over these pages and use whatever you may learn here in your own life and work.

When I first set out to produce this book, I found that my travels were the best way to organize the photographs and text. Why? Because I realized that my work was my education, and everything I did added to my knowledge. Every job change was an effort to graduate to new challenges, more knowledge. For that reason, I felt the need to tell not only the story behind the photographs, but also explain the reasons for my frequent career changes.

In short, this book may appear to be a "Photo Book," but it is not. The text is equally important to explain the inexplicable peculiarities of life and journalism.

Full disclosure: I always found it difficult to read and write. I flunked grade school and dropped out of college. Finally, I discovered that I was dyslexic! What to do? I found a home in the army for two years and taught myself to touch type, learned vocabulary by reading Joseph Conrad, and later managed to finish college. Only then did I realized that my real educational path was to explore the world through journalism.

Enjoy the book!

Searching for Music Temple

Three of us set off in the fall of 1965 to explore the side canyons of Southern Utah's Colorado River. These Navaho tribal lands were dotted with Anasazi cliff dwellings and other architectural treasures. More important for us, however, was our search for a place of exceptional beauty called Music Temple, a majestic grotto named by the Colorado River explorer John Wesley Powell in 1869.

I traveled with Colorado newspaper publisher Bil* Dunaway and Aspen artist David Michael. All of us were rock climbers and had no trouble scaling the steep canyon walls using what were called "mokie steps" cut into the sandstone by the ancients.

Music Temple and the Anasazi ruins were doomed by the rising waters of Lake Powell, which had begun filling two years before when construction of the Glen Canyon Dam blocked the Colorado River at Page, Arizona. The dam was built despite strong protests from environmentalists, who had fought to save the important architectural and natural treasures in the area.

When we finally found Music Temple, we realized that one of the wonders of the world was about to be lost. To grasp the scale of these walls, look for the tiny human figure in the sand below the grotto's dome. This may be one of the last photographs of Music Temple before it was drowned by the waters of Lake Powell.

If you haven't yet read Edward Abbey's *The Monkey Wrench Gang* about this environmental battleground, it is worthy of your effort.

*This is the way Bil spelled his name.

AT RIGHT: To comprehend the size of Music Temple, look for the tiny human figure in the sand below the grotto's dome. When the waters of Lake Powell flooded Music Temple, a wonder of the world was lost.

Bil Dunaway Takes a Chance

Bil* Dunaway is steering our skiff upriver after our visit to Music Temple. Bil, editor of *The Aspen Times*, was renowned in Colorado for his award-winning editorials supporting civil rights and clean government – and the environment. I can only imagine what editorial he was writing in his mind when I snapped this picture. Bil published *The Aspen Times* for almost 40 years beginning in 1956. He died February 25, 2011 at the age of 87.

Backing up a bit: It is extremely difficult for someone with no journalistic experience to get a newspaper job. After college I had driven to Colorado to find employment. I knew the state of Colorado fairly well because of my Aunt Betsy Cowles. A mountain climber living in Colorado Springs, she had hiked in the Rocky Mountains with my family for several summers. In 1959 newspaper jobs were almost impossible to find, in part because a national wire service had just folded leaving many experienced journalists job hunting.

My job interviews would go like this: "What is your newspaper experience?" Answer: None. "Unfortunately, we can't hire you with no experience." I asked how I could get experience if no one would hire me? "Good question," was the usual reply. Another of life's interesting dilemmas!

One day I drove up the Roaring Fork Valley to Aspen and located *The Aspen Times*. Inside I found Bil Dunaway typing away in his tiny, cluttered cubical. I asked Bil for a job as a reporter. He politely informed me that he already had a full staff. I asked Bil if he knew about the airplane accident at the airport. No, he did not. I asked him a few other questions about the area and he agreed to put me to work, half-time.

I owe a lot to the man who gave me my first newspaper job.

* In case you missed it, this is the way Bil spelled his name.

AT RIGHT: On Lake Powell, a pensive Bil Dunaway composes a future editorial after visiting the soon-to-be-submerged Music Temple.

Carbondale, Colorado

Not long after I joined *The Aspen Times*, Bil asked me to help him launch a new weekly down the Roaring Fork Valley in Glenwood Springs. We named it *The Glenwood Sage* and I soon became its inexperienced but full-time editor.

Working on a new weekly in an old Colorado town was not particularly easy. First, we were in competition with a well-established weekly named *The Glenwood Post*. They were venerable, experienced, and definitely "insiders." We at *The Sage* were "outsiders," plus I was new at the job. That made for a very interesting experience.

Joe Koller, a talented advertising man, kept the paper rolling with nicely designed ads and I would fill the weekly papers with news and editorials. To get the paper printed, we would drive our copy up to *The Aspen Times* for typesetting and printing. The ancient printing press at *The Times* had been hauled over Independence Pass on a sledge in the late 1800s. We would load up the press, feed it single sheets of newsprint, and throw buckets of water around the floor to ward off dreaded static electricity. It was exciting work. Our skilled printer, named "Blue," once rigged up a soft drink bottle filled with red ink, plugged it with a cork and a pipe cleaner which fed a bold red line down the edge of page one, making our competition fret about how we had "achieved color."

AT RIGHT: There is something heartening about seeing these three old-timers joined in friendship and conversation at Carbondale, Colorado's Annual Potato Days Festival. This photo was taken in the 1960s.

Bet on the Greased Pig

Personally, I would not like to be a greased pig, and I doubt if the animal rights people would support a greased pig race today. This photo was taken in the 1960s at the Annual Potato Days Festival in Carbondale, Colorado, where just about every youngster in the county did their best to do the impossible – catch a very speedy and extremely slippery, greased, four-legged, open-field running pig who almost always leaves two-legged pursuers in the dust.

Until I looked through my own work, I did not realize that the photographs we take today, and the news stories we write, become the history of tomorrow. The physical landscape of our towns and cities changes over time in the same way that our personal landscape changes.

These children chasing the greased pig are all grown up now, and the cowboys on the previous page may no longer be with us. I have not visited the Carbondale fairgrounds since I took these photos, but most communities have changed radically in the past 50 years and Carbondale is probably no exception.

After about a year at *The Glenwood Sage*, I realized I needed to learn much more about reporting and writing, and also about photography. So, I packed up my things and headed to Louisville, Kentucky, my birthplace.

AT RIGHT: Children scamper after the elusive pig at the annual event in Carbondale. It is almost impossible to best a greased, open-field running pig.

Louisville, Kentucky

While visiting Louisville, I dropped by the personnel department of *The Louisville Times*, and using my clippings from the Colorado weekly, I applied for a job. Fortunately, there was a vacancy. The previous picture page editor had just left for a job with *National Geographic*. I was offered his position and I accepted. Suddenly, everything I wanted to know and needed to learn was there waiting for me.

On my first day of work at *The Times*, I learned that the daily "Picture Page" was the personal fiefdom of the Managing Editor, Norman Isaacs. My job as editor of the picture page was to come up with the ideas, clear them with "Mr. Isaacs," get a photographer assigned from the Photo Department, accompany him or her on the "shoot," take the resulting prints into the boss, watch him whip through them like a tornado, tossing out the ones he rejected, piling up the ones he liked, then sending me on my way to the Graphics Department for layout.

After that I was free to write the text, have the engraving department and back shop transform the photos and text into lead, and make up the page for proofing. And it was always good to have two or three pages ready in advance.

One very early morning my phone rang. It was Norman Isaacs. "Smith, we need a picture page on Roger Maris TODAY!" "Yes, sir, Mr. Isaacs." I got right on it, drove to the office, asked the first person I met: "Who the hell is Roger Maris?" The library provided photos, I wrote glowingly about what's-his-name, the new home-run king. The boss was pleased.

AT RIGHT: Professional wrestling is primarily "entertainment" and I occasionally attended these matches mostly out of curiosity. Is this profession a fraud? Possibly, probably, but all the same these men look genuinely concerned.

Inside a Big City Newsroom

Working for *The Louisvillle Times* was much different than the Colorado weekly. I was on the fourth floor of a huge corporate building. The newsroom extended across an entire block. *The Times* was on one side, and separated by a glass partition were the reporters of *The Louisville Courier-Journal*, our sister paper. They were the morning paper; we were the afternoon paper. They were the older paper with many Pulitzer Prizes to their credit. We considered ourselves, not superior to our friendly rivals, but more feisty and hard-hitting.

We numbered a dozen or more, each had a desk, typewriter, telephone, plenty of copy paper and a paste pot to glue our copy together. Needless to say, this was before the computer era.

On my far right, close to the wire service room, was the amazing Richard Harwood, crack political reporter, usually on the phone with his feet up on his desk. Richard later became Ombudsman for *The Washington Post*. On my left was a new intern, Charlayne Hunter (now Charlayne Hunter-Gault), developing her reporting skills before becoming a shining star for Public Broadcasting and reporting from Africa.

One of my favorite writers at *The Times* was John Fetterman, a man of few words when he was not writing. Every morning when I entered the newsroom, I would pass John's desk and he would look up and say three words: "Good morning, John." And I would reply the same. John was given the assignment to write a front-page story of President John Kennedy's ground breaking for the Louisville post office, directly across the street from us. John's story concentrated on giving instructions to the president, who had serious back pain, on how to properly use a shovel. I learned a lot from John Fetterman.

AT RIGHT: I was given the assignment to attend a revival in Louisville and determine if fraud was involved. I decided it was not, but it can be heart breaking when a call for healing goes unanswered.

13

Clean Copy, Please!

After learning everything I could about photo editing, caption writing, and picture page editing, I joined the ranks of Staff Writers at *The Times*, and that is when one really learns to produce "clean copy." Here is how it works. You write a news story and it goes to the Copy Desk. The head of the desk assigns it to a Copy Editor. If your copy is "clean" – without errors or other problems – you won't see it again until it is in print. If it is returned to you with notations, you make the necessary changes and send it back. If it is returned to you too often, well, you will be out of a job. This leads to rapid learning. The Copy Desk is the best writing teacher of all.

Among my various assignments as a staff writer was the early morning task of covering the track at Churchill Downs before the big Kentucky Derby race. I was asked to interview early ticket seekers, some of whom had spent the night waiting in line. Using a public telephone, I would dictate my story to a reporter for an early edition of the newspaper. Since my work was over by post time, instead of attending my first Kentucky Derby, I drove to a local hospital to walk my wife Katy around the halls until it was time to welcome our son Nicholas into the world. To this day Nicholas, now living in California, celebrates his Kentucky Derby birthday according to Louisville's local custom, with mint juleps.

AT RIGHT: I have no idea if the horse getting washed down in this photo was destined to be a Derby winner, and since I was not a *Times* photographer, I didn't really care. I was free to shoot whatever I wanted, and, clearly, I was more interested in racetrack laundry than the race.

Three Accomplished Pros

While at *The Louisville Times*, I once witnessed our managing editor, Norman Isaacs, in the middle of a deadline emergency. Two reporters had mistakenly been assigned to report the same major event, and both stories went to the Copy Desk at the same time as the deadline loomed. From his office nearby, our boss heard the resulting commotion. He quickly ascertained the problem, sat down at the nearest typewriter, instructed the two reporters to stand on opposite sides of him and tell him their stories at the same time while he typed out a single story from the two narratives. He then sent the copy to the Copy Desk just in time for the deadline. That was Mr. Isaacs at his best, at work under pressure.

While editing the picture page, I frequently requested a young photographer named Bill Strode to shoot the assignment because of his great ability. In a way, I learned to see through his eyes while working with him. This deepened my respect for photography. Later, as a free-lancer, Bill worked for *Time, Life, National Geographic, The New York Times*, and *The Washington Post*. He was named Photographer of the Year in 1966. He deserved it.

AT RIGHT: This is Harvey Sloane, a college friend who taught me to ride freight trains. We would climb aboard an empty car and ride through the night wondering where we would end up. After college Harvey went to medical school, then moved to Louisville where he became Mayor of the city. On this day, we had borrowed a boat to go exploring on one of Kentucky's many lakes.

Getting Ready to Ride

At a motorcycle rally in Louisville my camera caught two contestants doing whatever motorcycle men do when waiting their turn to ride.

Hitchhiking to Somewhere

Leaving Louisville, an unknown soldier hitchhiked in the rain,
hoping for a ride over the Ohio River Bridge to Indiana or beyond.

On to Middletown, New York

I had been fortunate to be able to follow my own path in my work. I learned everything I wanted to know in Louisville – how to write, photograph, create picture page layouts. Then I moved on to a new job that allowed me to be both a reporter and a photographer and to lay out my own picture pages. *The Times-Herald Record* in Middletown, New York, was one of the first "offset" newspapers in the U.S. That meant stunning reproduction of photos compared to the older method of printing.

Also, *The Record* had a rule that all reporters must carry cameras and know how to use them. There was no "photo department" as such at this daily paper, although there was an excellent photographer, Manny Fuchs. *The Record* was also known for hiring aspiring young Turks like the late Hunter S. Thompson, also from Louisville, who was reportedly fired for kicking in the candy machine when it failed to deliver his order.

Full disclosure: I had an inside tract to *The Record*, although I'm not certain it was necessary. Jim Ottaway, my close friend and college roommate, worked there as a reporter and his father owned the newspaper. At my new job, I had more freedom, longer hours, more satisfaction, and a "life change."

AT RIGHT: I snapped this photo in the industrial section of Louisville. It represents my feelings about "work," meaning lots to do, and often little pleasure in the doing. This may be unfair to this man. He may have loved his job, and I hope he did. My wish for everyone, whenever possible, is for you to follow your passion and love what you are doing. My grandfather used the phrase "He adorned his profession." That was the era before "he" or "she."

Spell of a Bygone Era

For a picture page, it is always desirable to capture one photo that tells the essence of a story, like this image of a father and his son caught in the spell of a bygone era. "Nothing is prouder of its age than an antique car" was my lead for a picture page on vintage cars in Monroe, New York. I enjoyed my new freedom at *The Record*.

Revolutionary Sport

There is something marvelously touching about this modern-day sharpshooter who is searching the feet of his British adversary for evidence of damage.

In Search of the Invisible

While working at *The Record* in Middletown, I requested a two-week assignment to investigate and report on the largely invisible effects of poverty in Orange County, New York.

I spent that time combing remote rural areas for traces of those who were off the grid, off welfare, and living hand-to-mouth in the cold of winter. When I found them, I talked with them, and, when appropriate, photographed them, then wrote about their lives.

A young boy had been hauling drinking water from a nearby stream and his footprints in the snow led me to a cold, dilapidated house occupied by a family of six. On leaving the house, I happened to turn and notice this young girl gazing out the window – a reflection of the bleakness of the season as well as her future.

This photo ran daily in the week-long series on poverty in Orange County and the young girl became an unwitting, disturbing poster girl for poverty in New York State. My story might have been a significant one for the newspaper, but Robert Van Fleet, Chief of *Ottaway News Service*, added to the story by covering Lyndon Johnson's War on Poverty in the U.S and the series became a blockbuster. Al Romm, editor of *The Record*, called the series "monumental and stirring."

But that was 1964. Today, in the New Century, there are still people living on or over the edge. Sometimes hungry, some times freezing, some without any shelter at all. Some are physically ill, some mentally ill, some addicted, some are just out of a job. What can we do about this?

AT RIGHT: An unnamed child with a bleak future became an unwitting poster girl for poverty in this series for *The Times-Herald Record* in Middletown, N.Y.

Meeting the President

President John F. Kennedy was planning to dedicate the Pinchot Institute for Conservation Studies in a rural area outside Milford, Pennsylvania on Tuesday, September 24, 1963. Our newspaper was many miles away in neighboring New York State, but I felt it important that we travel to that event.

We arrived early, just before the presidential helicopter from Washington touched down in a nearby field. I took some photographs of the president, as well as Interior Secretary Stewart Udall, before the two of them rode in a convertible up to the Gifford Pinchot house. I headed through a nearby rhododendron thicket, up a hill, and came out on a secluded flagstone walkway bordering the house. I was alone, except for the man walking toward me. It was the President. He, too, was alone, headed for the outdoor amphitheater where he would speak. He was relaxed, pleasant. He greeted me and asked how I was.

Three months after this event, we learned that President Kennedy had been shot and killed in Dallas, Texas, while riding in a motorcade with his wife.

My earlier meeting with the President had, in some deep way, affected my internal compass. Now he was dead. My heart was heavy for his family and the nation, but I was also filled with the sense that life was too short, that I needed to make a radical change in my life. I soon left my job, packed up, loaded my family into a 24-foot travel trailer and headed West, toward the unknown.

AT RIGHT: The President, flanked by a Secret Service man in dark glasses, signs autographs at the Pinchot Institute near Milford, Pennsylvania, three months before he was assassinated in Dallas, Texas.

Addressing the crowd at the Pinchot Institute in September 1963, President Kennedy
called for an all-out effort to conserve America's natural resources.

Our June Bug

This is Emily, our June Bug, the newest member of our family. She was born on June 5, 1963, in Goshen, New York, three months before I met the President. I took this photograph of Emily several years later, in our pickup truck in Little Woody Creek, Colorado. Today, at age 50, Emily still has that look and that big heart.

Freelancing in the West

Lyndon Johnson, President Kennedy's vice president, took over the presidency after Kennedy's assassination in 1963. It was a troubling time for the country, both because of the assassination and because of our continued involvement in the unpopular Vietnam War.

I was somewhat adrift, searching for my next challenge. I tried freelance work, traveling the West and developing film in our travel trailer. I found it difficult not having a home base.

Once I was parked in Jackson Hole, Wyoming, when the new president's wife, Lady Bird Johnson, was in the area with Washington dignitaries, including Secretary of the Interior Stewart Udall. I photographed both at a banquet in Jackson.

Frankly I do not recall the reason for this event, but a raft trip down the Snake River was an important part of it. The national press was well represented (*National Geographic, Life, Time,* etc.), but it happened that *My Curious Camera* was the only medium chosen to represent the "local press." Thus my Pentax and I were the only "press" allowed to accompany Lady Bird and Secretary Udall down the river.

What became of this remarkable "scoop?" Lady Bird used my camera to take a few photos on the river trip, and I mailed those to her. Then my efforts to sell the story and remaining photographs failed. So, you, the reader, have this exclusive especially for yourself.

There is a second "scoop" for you on the next page, from a trip to Arizona. I'm not even sure if I ever sent that story out. Finally, I solved my shortcomings as a freelancer by moving back to the Roaring Fork Valley in Colorado. There I worked on a book about Aspen, wrote for another weekly newspaper, and built fences.

AT RIGHT: Lady Bird Johnson, then the nation's First Lady, attends a banquet in Jackson, Wyoming, with Interior Secretary Stewart Udall. What was Lady Bird like? She was absolutely Divine!

A Cobbler's Tale

This is George Clark in his dusty shoe shop in Patagonia, Arizona (population 550 at that time), and here is what he had to say.

"For seven years I packed supplies to my friend who was outlawed back in Oklahoma. I toted 100 pounds of flour and ammunition and the like for forty miles back into the mountains so he could stay hid out with his brother. As long as you had ammo, you could live as long as you pleased in those hills.

"Stevens was the name of my friend. He used to be a U.S. Marshall in the Oklahoma Indian Territory about 1909, but he refused to take bribes from the whiskey runners. One night at a dance there was a killing and someone yelled, 'Stevens done it!' So, he had to run.

"He waded 90 miles up the South Canadian River to throw off the bloodhounds and he hid out in the Kiamichi Mountains for seven years until the government finally broke up the bootleggers. After that, Stevens walked out of the hills and no one laid a hand on him.

"I was about 18 then, and I thought a lot of Stevens. He was sort of like a hero to me, so I kept him supplied while he was outlawed."

A month later I again passed through Patagonia. The rusted sign was still there, but the doors and windows of the old shoe shop were boarded up. A waitress in the nearby café said she thought the old cobbler had simply closed up shop. She didn't know where he lived. Maybe he had left town or gone back into the mountains.

AT RIGHT: George Clark spent seven years supplying an honorable friend who was running from the law in Oklahoma.

Dreams and Dilemmas

I discovered that freelancing as a journalist was not a successful enterprise for me, so I returned to Aspen and began working on a book with local writer Peggy Clifford. One crisp winter morning I took this shot of Aspen's early architecture with its backdrop of a steep, snow-covered mountain.

Peggy and I used this photo for the cover of the book, *Aspen, Dreams and Dilemmas*, the story, in pictures and prose, of the future of America's small towns. Some towns were withering away, others were gobbled up by expanding cities. Aspen became a victim of its own success and the beauty of its location, threatened by the corrosive effects of speculation and development.

Peggy, an accomplished writer, worked on the book's text, while I laid out the pages and edited illustrations both from historical archives and from the work of local photographers, including myself. It took us years to produce the book or so it seemed. And we were fortunate to have found a publisher interested in western history, The Swallow Press of Chicago.

Those interested in the financial side of producing a book might want to know that Peggy and I made about three cents an hour for our labors. Our book was soon "remaindered" because it did not excite a national following. (At that time books "remaining" in publisher's stock after sales had declined were sold at reduced prices.) Recently a friend from Aspen reported that one of our books was now selling locally for over $300, while a used bookstore in Denver offered the same book for $45. Interesting.

The charm of the Roaring Fork Valley as well as its geographic isolation drew me back to the area time and again. Also the very quirky and interesting people who were attracted to the area appealed to me. You will meet some of these characters in the following pages.

AT RIGHT: The snowy cornice of an old Aspen building in front of the imposing slopes of Aspen Mountain provided the cover photograph for our book about the future of small towns in America.

A Close Call

David Hiser is an elusive mountain man who prefers to live above 8,000 feet. David was my early morning hiking companion when I lived in the mountains of Colorado. He became an accomplished *National Geographic* photographer and, besides other assignments, he accompanied an archaeological expedition into the jungles of Guatemala in 1985. The Guatemalan army had brutally repressed local rebels and driven them into the jungle where they encountered David and the expedition's archaeologist. Facing M-16 rifles, David explained their peaceful mission. Fortunately, they were allowed to continue down the Usumacinta River, happy to be alive.

Man of Iron

I was now back in the community where I began my journalism career. I worked for a time on stories and picture pages for the *Aspen Illustrated News*. This was the lead photo on a story called "Man of Iron" about Francis Whitaker, a brilliant wrought-iron artist, an inspiring teacher, and eloquent labor leader. Francis produced beautiful work, but nothing revealed his strength and ability with tools more than his muscular hands and forearms.

Francis received the Colorado Governor's Award for Excellence in the Arts in 1995 and the National Heritage Fellowship from the National Endowment for the Arts in 1997. He died in Glenwood Springs, Colorado in 1999.

Violet Ray Returns

This is Paul Semonin, photographed in his $500 cabin on Smuggler Mountain, Pitkin County, Colorado. Paul, a.k.a. Violet Ray, has flown below the radar most of his life – until he was recently discovered living in Eugene, Oregon by the University of Oregon's Art Museum staff of the same city. The museum then exhibited Paul's ground-breaking anti-war and anti-corporate graphics and invited Paul to give a Gallery Talk about his collages from the 1960s. Paul's most recent works include clandestine projections with timely Occupy Wall Street messages on public buildings, plus his thought-provoking bumper stickers that read "Mastodon Nation."

I looked closely at my proof sheet for this photo and recognized, in the following frame, Paul's old friend from Louisville, Hunter S. Thompson, coddling a morning cup of potent liquid. Paul had just returned from Ghana, Africa. Hunter was then living in Woody Creek, down valley from Paul.

When the snow melted at Aspen's 8,000 feet and the frozen land thawed and the fields again turned green, I returned to my early occupation of working on the land. This time it was repairing fences up Little Woody Creek with Storrs Bishop, Brad Bingham, and "Whisper." Each of us was wrestling with the question of what to do with our lives. Storrs decided that he wanted to be a veterinarian. "Whisper" thought he would make a good public school teacher, and I was toying with the idea of getting a Master's degree so I could teach journalism. Brad, who had once worked for a bank in the East, thought that manual labor was much more satisfying than banking, so he kept building fences. Storrs, "Whisper," and I drove to Boulder and signed up for programs at the University of Colorado.

AT RIGHT: Graphic artist Paul Semonin working in his Colorado mountain cabin after his return from Ghana, Africa.

Where Are We, Please?

At the University of Colorado I signed up for the newly created graduate program in journalism, which would give me a ticket to teach at the college level – if I could find employment.

The subject of my Master's thesis was the editorial department of *The Denver Post*, which I chose because of the shadowy, elusive nature of that department in many daily newspapers. I found myself spending most of my time at *The Post* with political cartoonist Pat Oliphant. In his small office he taught me how to accurately shoot rubber bands. His target of choice was a photograph of a former president of the United States, who shall remain nameless. With both his pen and his rubber bands, Pat Oliphant was a keen shot.

A native of Adelaide, Australia, Pat won the Pulitzer Prize for his political cartoons in 1967, a year after this photograph, opposite, was taken. *The New York Times* recently called Pat Oliphant "the most influential editorial cartoonist now working."

I spent two semesters at CU at this time. All the while, I later learned, I was on "academic probation" due to my untimely departure as a freshman 14 years earlier – impetuous youth volunteers for the draft!

With the backing of Department Chairman Jim Brinton and Professor Gayle Waldrop, I applied for an opening at UCLA. I was flown to Los Angeles for an interview shortly before my graduation. I met with students, gave a talk about offset printing, and later went to lunch with the faculty. During the meal, I leaned over to the only faculty member wearing a work shirt. He was William Weber Johnson, a former *Time-Life* reporter and author of the marvelous book *Heroic Mexico*. I asked him a simple question that had been bothering me since my flight to Los Angeles. "Pardon my ignorance, but could you tell me the name of that large body of water that we flew over while landing at LAX?" The answer came quickly. "Of course, John, that was the Pacific Ocean." I was learning fast. And believe it or not, I got the job.

AT RIGHT: Political cartoonist Pat Oliphant working at *The Denver Post* before winning his Pulitzer Prize in 1967.

41

Teaching in Los Angeles

Teaching journalism was very different than "doing" journalism. And, frankly, at first I wondered if I had bitten off more than I could chew. I was teaching in a graduate school, which meant smaller classes than the crowded undergraduate world at UCLA.

We taught basic reporting techniques in a classroom set up as a newsroom with a copy desk. Students published a weekly newspaper, *The California Sun*, in the department's print shop down the hall. Besides assisting Bill Johnson and Jim Howard with the reporting lab, I operated a darkroom and taught photography and graphic arts classes. And that would have been fine if I had been comfortable in the role of "Teacher." A journalist can survive very well as an introvert. A successful photographer can be "a fly on the wall," a writer can quietly ask questions, then write with authority, but a "Professor" is a very visible dude, and I wanted to hide.

Los Angeles has a very common solution to such problems: the psychiatrist. So, I went to one for a few sessions. He was a Freudian, meaning he seldom spoke. Neither did I. It was more comfortable for me to teach than continue those silent sessions. So, I soon gave up on therapy and simply overcame my own shyness.

Teaching was exciting because each year brought brighter students and new challenges that required frequent changes in my own attitudes – and the media itself was changing rapidly. Television news, for example, was quickly expanding. For that reason, our department launched a division to train journalists for television news and documentaries.

AT RIGHT: This is our son Nicholas, hard at work in the sand near Long Beach after our drive from Colorado. Today this energetic, creative lad is a whirling dervish in Silicon Valley. How quickly this transformation happens!

Young Woman in the Office

This is Yolanda. She worked in the Journalism Department at UCLA while I was teaching there. She was quiet, low in the pecking order, and almost invisible. I snapped this photo of her one afternoon, printed it up in the darkroom, and posted it on the bulletin board.

"She's beautiful, who is she?" I was asked.

"That's Yolanda," I answered. "She works in our office."

After that Yolanda became more visible, and had many more visitors. It's interesting how one photograph can create unforeseen changes.

Young Man in the City

While working in the city, I was in the habit of spending Sunday mornings with young lads from an East Los Angeles orphanage. I would drive them to local parks or the coast to take photographs and to spend some time out-of-doors. I would print up their photos and hand them over at our next outing. This young man was a regular, and made a strong impression on me. He was serious, thoughtful, and I held him in high regard.

Recent efforts to contact him through the state education system have been unsuccessful. I do wonder what he made of his life after the orphanage, and how he is faring. Losing contact is one of the human losses we often sustain when we need to make personal changes.

War on the Home Front

And now a bit of history. The 1960s were a time of change. It was also a time of rebellion against an older structure and a time of experimentation with new forms by a younger generation – new forms in art, dress, music, media, and, yes, even sex.

The war in Vietnam, and the reaction against it, turned this country's campuses, including UCLA where I worked, into a sort of "battleground." Some universities, including ours, became a national magnet for sometimes violent activists. Governor Ronald Reagan locked down the UCLA campus shortly after his car was pelted with eggs following a campus meeting of university chancellors.

Classes were cancelled, students were on strike, and police manned the rooftops with their weapons. And it was not long before the budgetary axe crashed down on the campus. Particularly hard hit was journalism. Why? Because journalists were carriers of "all the bad news" from Vietnam, making them hugely unpopular. It was crystal clear to me that our department, which had recently moved into television journalism, was going to go nowhere in the future. So I decided to move on. After five productive years at UCLA, I gave notice to my department and prepared to move my family back to Colorado.

I did two things before leaving California. I had written an academic paper stressing the need for local, citizen-run communications to offset the power of the national media. Also, I had purchased a Sony portable half-inch video camera and recorder, one of the earliest to arrive in the United States. I understood that this portable camera – long before the development of present day hand-held video cameras and cell phones – might revolutionize media by permitting regular citizens to produce news clips or even television programs of their own.

I told a commercial TV station owner about my intention to start a community station in Colorado using portable equipment. "That would be impossible," he told me. I am forever grateful for his response because that was all the motivation I needed.

GrassRoots community television in Colorado is now approaching its 50th year.

AT RIGHT: In a control room at UCLA, students in the new TV-Journalism program work on "The Bitter Inheritance," their hour-long documentary about the Vietnam War. An excellent book about journalists and the Vietnam War is *Once Upon a Distant War* by William Prochnau.

Little Woody Creek

I was looking forward to the challenge of launching something perhaps never before undertaken, creating a non-profit, volunteer community television station. It was something I knew absolutely nothing about. So where to begin?

During summers, our family had been slowly building a cabin up Little Woody Creek, down river from Aspen, Colorado. Aspen had a radio station, but no local television, only imported television signals via a local cable. It was a perfect location for a community station. I named it GrassRoots.

A string of talented volunteers appeared, eager for media experience: David W., Candi, Linda, Richie, Shelley, Randy, Dan, Katy, Andy, Jeff, Ed, David H., Maura, James, Buddy, and dozens and dozens more – you know who you are!

I was fortunate to have an unsung mentor during the early years of GrassRoots. Edgar Stanton was his name. When I was faced with an unusually difficult problem I would call on Edgar. He would order sandwiches and we would sit in his home on Red Mountain and talk it through. I don't know what I would have done without him.

The program that really got GrassRoots rolling was our homegrown soap opera named "The Edge of Ajax" – Ajax being the name of the mountain that bordered the town. The soap opera production, about Aspen's zany present and its mining past, ran throughout the summer of 1972. It created instant fans for community theater on cable television.

AT RIGHT: Over many summers, and with the help of friends, we built a cabin up Little Woody Creek. We started with an outhouse and kerosene lamps, then graduated to electricity and plumbing. We moved back to Little Woody Creek permanently in 1971. This was a view from the cabin.

GrassRoots Takes Root

My GrassRoots experience in Colorado lasted seven years and was one of the most interesting and challenging periods of my life. We developed a skilled staff that trained summer interns from colleges throughout the United States. The city loaned us office space, the cable company donated studio space, the federal government's CETA program (Comprehensive Employment and Training Act) funded educational training for our workshops, local businesses provided sponsorships that supported our productions, and viewers donated the funds to keep our non-profit solvent.

GrassRoots provided local news, including election coverage, public access for all citizens, documentaries, special events, live conferences on ecology, the economy, food, women's issues, and coverage of county commissioners' meetings. We even traveled over the mountains to Denver to cover action by the state legislature.

We also earned a place in the intern program of New York University's Alternate Media Center, headed by George Stoney. We helped launch the National Association of Cable Programmers that gave community access stations like ours legal standing to defend our rights, testify in court, etc.

After seven years at the helm, I finally achieved "burn out," and sought less demanding pastures.

Since that time GrassRoots has had many reincarnations as new leaders have emerged to take over and steer it in new directions. At the present time, the community station is managed by John Masters, a documentary filmmaker who, among other achievements, has expanded GrassRoots coverage down valley to Carbondale.

My own path took me in entirely new directions. I divorced, moved West, bought a small farm in Oregon where I have lived contentedly with my wife Catherine for the past 35 years, raising vegetables, adopting stray animals, splitting wood, building small structures, aging busily, and giving thanks for good friends and many blessings.

Remembering Ajax

Ajax was my constant companion after leaving Colorado and driving West – once again into the unknown. I always spoke to Ajax normally, as a friend. If I parked and was going into a store to buy a newspaper and some toothpaste, I would tell him those details. He listened to every word. And he seemed to know me better than I knew myself. I was once rock climbing too fast and too high, and Ajax knew it. He barked at me non-stop until I came to my senses and retraced my steps.

Ajax had a natural nobility. He sat up proudly in the passenger seat of my pickup truck. He knew how to draw people over to him if he wanted to meet them. He treated lesser dogs with patient disdain. He was a bit jealous at times, and would completely ignore a female dog if I complimented the dog to its owner. Ajax was actually my touchstone, and, as I used to say, "my better half."

Ajax was always with me, until one day he wasn't. I had flown with him to Kentucky and we were exploring the family farm. I called to him, and for the first time ever, he didn't appear. I found him lying near a stream. He had died in the prime of his life. I carried his body up the hill, dug his grave near the house and buried him.

I have been fortunate to have had many fine dogs, but none like Ajax. He was the King of Dogs, and he took care of me when I needed it most.

The Cover Story

Fast forward to the past. I was passing through New York City in 1960 on my way back to my first newspaper job in Colorado. Curious about the city's huge public library, I entered, and snapped this one photo in the foyer.

The image raises a dozen questions. Was there a connection between the man and the lovely nun? What had the nun found in the glass case? Was the man-in-motion seeking "Shelter?" Lastly, is this photograph prophetic? Was he, in fact, *me*? Full disclosure: The previous day I had been married in a Catholic church to Katy in Cooperstown, New York. Our marriage produced two fine children and ended in divorce.

This photograph seems to be, in the words of French photographer Cartier-Bresson, a "Decisive Moment." If you haven't seen his photographic book by that name, you might seek it out.

It is unforgettable.

52